31 Days with God
FOR FATHERS

BARBOUR
PUBLISHING

Material taken and adapted from *Wisdom from the Proverbs* by Dan and
Nancy Dick.

ISBN 978-1-60260-018-8

All scripture quotations are taken from the King James Version of the
Bible.

Published by Barbour Publishing, Inc., P.O. Box 719, Uhrichsville,
Ohio 44683, www.barbourbooks.com

*Our mission is to publish and distribute inspirational products offering
exceptional value and biblical encouragement to the masses.*

Member of the
Evangelical Christian
Publishers Association

Printed in the United States of America.

HONOR THY FATHER

My son, hear the instruction of thy father,
and forsake not the law of thy mother.
PROVERBS 1:8

Parents are entrusted with an awesome responsibility. The idea of raising a child or instructing a young boy or girl in the best way to live is incredible. Hundreds of times in their lives, every mother and father questions the decisions they make. The ongoing prayer of most men and women is that they make good choices for their children. Their consolation comes from their children's happiness and prosperity. When the Bible says that children should honor their parents, it is saying that children should live in such a way that no dishonor will befall their mothers and fathers.

This is also true of our relationship with our heavenly Father. God wants only the best for us. He has given instruction not to show His power or might, but to help us live the best life we can. He only wants our peace and happiness. In turn, we should live in such a way that He is honored. Our actions should reflect the quality of our upbringing. We should live as proof of how much we love God.

Dear God, please assist us in our attempts to live as You have instructed. Help us to be a glory and an honor to You. May we do nothing to bring shame to Your holy name. Amen.

Nobody can acquire honor by
doing what is wrong.
THOMAS JEFFERSON

UNDERSTANDING GOD'S WILL

*My son, forget not my law; but let thine heart keep my
commandments: for length of days, and long life,
and peace, shall they add to thee.*

PROVERBS 3:1–2

It is easy to see the Bible as a book of "don'ts" rather than a book of "dos." The "Thou shalt nots" far exceed the "Thou shalts." This is not a way for God to control us, for there is nothing farther from His intention than that; it is merely a show of His great love for us that He offers these instructions in order to make our lives better. Our God is a God of order and sense. He knows infinitely more than we can ever hope to, and He shares His knowledge with us to help us through our lives.

If we can learn to be obedient to the will of God, we will find that life becomes a little easier to live and a lot more fulfilling. Life ceases to be such a struggle, and it becomes a joy. God sent Christ to fight the battle for us. He had become the victor—our victor. To His disciples Jesus said, "Peace I leave with you, my peace I give to you." He says the same to us. If we can learn to be more obedient to God, His peace and assurance will be ours throughout our entire lives.

Dear God, help me that I might learn to rest in Your peace. Life can be so difficult, and I know I cannot handle everything on my own. Be with me, guiding me, and helping me to follow Your commandments always. Amen.

Love is the greatest thing that God can give us, for He Himself is love; and it is the greatest thing we can give to God, for it will also give ourselves.

JEREMY TAYLOR

USING WHAT GOD GIVES US

My son, let not them depart from thine eyes:
keep sound wisdom and discretion: When thou liest
down, thou shalt not be afraid: yea, thou shalt
lie down, and thy sleep shall be sweet.

PROVERBS 3:21, 24

A doctor had been practicing medicine for a number of years, when he found that he couldn't sleep at night. After a long, successful career, the doctor suddenly felt that his work was futile and senseless. As hard as he tried, he could not save everyone he treated, and many of his patients never got any better. His early dreams of healing those who were in pain and suffering began to fail. Night after night he tossed and turned, struggling to make peace with what he felt was failure.

An understanding of God—and what God wants from us as His children—can help us to have calm nights. No human being can take responsibility for life and death. God gave life, and He is the ruler of all life. For some people, God has chosen to allow them to assist in the healing process. He has given men and women the minds and talents to save and sustain life, yet it is always God who ultimately makes the decision of who will live and who will die. Our responsibility is to use our gifts and talents to the best of our abilities. If we will try to do so, we can count on God's richest blessing.

Help me, Father, to utilize the wonderful gifts and graces that You have seen fit to grant me. Bless me as I attempt to be the best person I can be, the person You made me to be. Amen.

∾

God is a kind Father. He sets us all in the places where He wishes us to be employed; and that employment is truly our Father's business. He chooses work for every creature. . . . He gives us always strength enough and sense enough for what He wants us to do.

JOHN RUSKIN

DECISION-MAKING

Hear, ye children, the instruction of a father,
and attend to know understanding.
PROVERBS 4:1

Young people are so anxious to gain independence and make their own decisions. When it comes to staying out late, how to dress, what to eat, and who to associate with, teenagers want their independence. Learning to make these choices is a part of growing up and maturing, but it takes time to learn to make wise choices. It also takes help. Though young people often resist the guidance and advice of their parents, there is much to be learned from adults who have lived through many of the situations they will face.

We are often just like children when it comes to the instruction of our heavenly Father. There is no situation that He does not know about, yet we often resist His instruction or ignore His guidance. It is the wise person who learns to take sound advice. We grow in our ability to accept His instruction as we grow in faith. It is only as we grow older that we begin to appreciate the decisions our parents made on our behalf as we were growing up. It is also true that we fully appreciate the rules that God has made for us when we mature spiritually.

Dear God, at times I act like a child in my faith. Help me to receive Your instruction with an open heart and mind. Grant me the wisdom to know that You are always trying to help me grow and to keep me on the path that I should follow. Amen.

Knowledge is horizontal. Wisdom is vertical—
it comes down from above.

BILLY GRAHAM

SEEING GOD'S CREATION

Wisdom is the principal thing; therefore get wisdom:
and with all thy getting get understanding.
PROVERBS 4:7

There are a lot of wonderful things on this earth that God has given us to enjoy. We live in a beautiful world full of glorious trees, breathtaking mountains, immense oceans, fabulous sunsets, and so on. Nature is splendid. Bright, sunny mornings with the birds singing and the dew sparkling on the grass are truly a gift of God. It is when we look at the world through the eyes of God that we come to appreciate just how special it is.

Real wisdom is the knowledge of God and all His handiworks. We have been given life so that we may enjoy it. It is a gift from God. When we pursue God and a deeper knowledge of His will, we are seeking a deeper understanding of all creation. There is nothing greater that anyone can desire than to see this world of ours through the eyes of the Creator. In God's creation we can catch glimpses of God Himself. In prayer we need to remember to ask God to help us become wise as He is wise, and in so doing we will see beauty like we never knew it existed before, appreciating life in a new and full way.

O Lord, I want to learn to enjoy life as fully as I can. Open my eyes to see anew, with the eyes of Your divine love. Through Your wisdom I can hope to come to know the fullness of life and beauty of Your creation. I praise You in Your greatness, O Father. Amen.

God's fingers can touch nothing
but to mold it into loveliness.
GEORGE MACDONALD

THE RIGHT PATH

*Hear, O my son, and receive my sayings; and the years
of thy life shall be many. I have taught thee in the way
of wisdom; I have led thee in right paths.*

Many times I have heard parents lament, "What have I done wrong?" Parents are all too willing to take the blame when their children make poor choices or get themselves into trouble. Parents want so much for their children to succeed and have pleasant, carefree lives. That is why there is special joy in seeing children succeed. Mothers and fathers can feel pride and take some credit for their children when they do well. It is an honor to the parents of children who succeed, that they have done a good job of bringing them up. When parents take interest in their children and treat them with respect and care, they are giving them as great a gift as is possible.

Our heavenly Father has tried to instruct us in the ways that lead to eternal life. He has allowed us to make our own choices, though, and we must take responsibility for them, bad or good. It is His greatest wish that we follow the wisdom of His will. When we do so, it is to His glory as well as ours that we have learned well. By listening to our heavenly Father, our lives are enriched and the years of our lives will be multiplied.

O God, You have been such a loving Father. Forgive me that I have often ignored the instructions You have given me for my sake. Help me to follow Your will and remain steadfast in my commitment to You. Amen.

∽

Can we not follow His footsteps,
filled with His Spirit, to finish the task appointed,
with heart aglow and hurrying feet?
V. RAYMOND EDMAN

Treasures

Keep thy heart with all diligence;
for out of it are the issues of life.
Proverbs 4:23

Jesus said, "Where your treasure is, there will your heart be also" (Matthew 6:21). What we feel and believe are the truly precious and meaningful things in our lives. If we don't commit ourselves to what is good and right, then we are empty. Moral poverty occurs when we place things above relationships. Christ sent His disciples out into the world without possessions, but no one in history has known more wealth than those chosen men who walked with Jesus. It is when we choose to walk with Jesus that we find out what true riches are.

In today's world, it is easy to get distracted by so many things. Lifestyles are presented in magazines and on television that seem so appealing. The "good life" requires money, good looks, nice clothes, and the right car, the right house, the right mate. At least, that's what we're supposed to believe. But it is only when we can free ourselves from the pursuit of such things that we can begin to enjoy life the way God intended it. Money cannot buy happiness, nor can it bring us life. Christ brings us life, and He brings it most abundantly. He is the real treasure, and as long as our hearts remain with Him, our lives will truly be rich.

Dear Father, forgive me when I lose sight of what is really important in life. Help me to keep my eyes focused on Your truth. Enable me to show others that You are the real treasure in life. Amen.

All that we call human history—money, poverty, ambition, war, prostitution, classes, empires, slavery—[is] the long, terrible story of man trying to find something other than God which will make him happy.

C. S. Lewis

DAY 8

CLAIMING THE NAME

*Hear me now therefore, O ye children, and depart
not from the words of my mouth. Lest thou give thine
honour unto others, and thy years unto the cruel.*
PROVERBS 5:7, 9

Whether we know it or not, we are being watched. Whenever we claim to be something, people will watch to see whether we live up to it. Athletes are judged by their performances. Investors are valued for their ability to make big money. Policemen are judged by their abilities to perform well under fire. What is it that Christians are judged for?

When we call ourselves Christians, we are claiming to be mirror images of Christ for all the world to see. We are presenting ourselves as examples of what God had in mind when He put men and women on this earth. It is a presumptuous claim we make, and one that carries with it a great amount of responsibility. One of the greatest sins we can ever commit is to call ourselves Christians and then act in ways which are unacceptable in the sight of the Lord. We must continually study the Word of God and follow the instructions God has given to us, devoting ourselves to imitating Christ in all ways possible. When we fail to do so, we bring dishonor not only on ourselves but also on the entire Christian church.

I pray that I might learn to walk carefully in the steps of Jesus Christ, Almighty Father. Grant that I might be an honor to Your truth in all ways. Be with me to shine Your light through my life that others may see Your greatness. Amen.

No man, for any considerable period,
can wear one face to himself and another
to the multitude, without finally getting
bewildered as to which may be true.

NATHANIEL HAWTHORNE

THE BEST THING

*Let thy fountain be blessed: and rejoice with the wife
of thy youth. Let her be as the loving hind and pleasant
roe; let her breasts satisfy thee at all times; and be thou
ravished always with her love.*

PROVERBS 5:18–19

While walking along the beach one evening, I saw an elderly couple strolling on the boardwalk. The man was blind, and his wife was lovingly leading him along. Her hands were gnarled with arthritis, and her legs were swollen. Both people looked as though they had lived difficult lives. Despite this, I could see the love with which the woman looked upon her mate. I walked up to the couple and told them that I was struck with how much in love they looked. The woman appeared a little embarrassed, but her husband spoke right up and said, "We've been married fifty-two years. I could never have made it without her. When everything else goes bad, I know I've still got the best little woman in the world to love me."

That old gentleman knew the real secret of happiness. It is never in the things we have or don't have. It's not in what happens or doesn't happen to us. The best thing in life is love. Those who are lucky enough to find someone to share their lives with enjoy a special gift from God. But for every person, the love of God is very real and very much freely given. We can be happy because we can know we are loved. Praise God!

O Lord, giver of life and giver of love, though I am unworthy, I thank You for loving me so much. Help me to know Your love at all times, and grant that I might be able to always spread that love wherever I might go. Amen.

I am a little pencil in the hand of a writing God who is sending a love letter to the world.

MOTHER TERESA

GOD'S COMMANDMENTS

*My son, keep my words, and lay up my commandments
with thee. Keep my commandments, and live; and
my law as the apple of thine eye. Bind them upon thy
fingers, write them upon the table of thine heart.*

PROVERBS 7:1–3

There was a man who spent his days sitting by an old firehouse, telling stories to the neighborhood children. The youngsters would flock around the man to hear him tell of bygone days. One striking feature of the old gentleman was that around each of his fingers he had tied a different colored string. The children would ask what the strings were for, and the old man would say that each one was to remind him of something important. This was the way he remembered things. But for everyone who came to him, he had this to share:

"You don't need strings to remember the most important things. God gave us ten fingers and ten commandments, and if you keep one commandment on each finger, you'll never forget any of them."

The commandments of God should be as much a part of us as the fingers on our hands. If we take care to remind ourselves of the laws of God, they will be forever inscribed on the very "table" of our heart.

Lord, I continue to forget the things I should do.
Help me to remember what You would have me
do. I cannot hope to be the person You want me
to be without Your help. Amen.

I on Thy statutes meditate,
Though evil men deride;
Thy faithful Word is my delight,
My counselor and guide.
THE 1912 PSALTER

The Strength of Love

For whoso findeth me findeth life, and shall obtain favour of the LORD. But he that sinneth against me wrongeth his own soul: all they that hate me love death.
Proverbs 8:35–36

A young man sat trembling in the police station. He had been picked up for shoplifting and now he waited for his parents, who were on their way to take him home. Being arrested was frightening and embarrassing, but it wasn't half as bad as having to face his mother and father. As they burst through the door, the young man saw that his mother had been crying. He bowed his head in shame and awaited the fury to come from his parents. Instead, he felt his mother's arm wrap around his shoulders and his father's big, warm hand on top of his head. He looked up through tears and saw that both of his parents were watching him with love and concern.

The boy asked, "Aren't you angry with me? Why aren't you yelling at me?"

His mother spoke. "Honey, when you hurt, we only want to help you. You've done wrong, but that doesn't mean we stop loving you. What you did hurts us, but we'll work it out together."

God loves us every bit as much. No matter what happens, if we work to find God, we will find love we never thought possible.

Dear heavenly Father, I fall prey to so much temptation and sin. I am ashamed that I cannot do what You would like for me to do. Thank You for Your forgiveness and love, especially in times when I don't deserve it. Amen.

Live every day in the knowledge that He loves you and He is present within you, enabling you to do mighty things for His kingdom.

GEORGE BARNA

FOLLOWING THE MASTER

*Give instruction to a wise man, and he
will be yet wiser: teach a just man,
and he will increase in learning.*
PROVERBS 9:9

A college professor laid out his teaching philosophy on the first day of class: "If you will let me, I will teach you as much as I can in these few short weeks, but if you resist me, I guarantee that you will learn nothing. You won't like everything I tell you, but if you will follow my instructions, you will leave here much better thinkers than when you came in."

The professor was a taskmaster who demanded perfection from his students. Many students, too lazy to put forth the proper effort, lost interest and complained about the strict grading and harsh comments. The few truly dedicated students found their professor to be one of the finest they ever had, and they valued his opinion above all others. This man helped them to be better than they thought possible.

God offers us the same kind of deal. If we will be open to His leadership, He will help us to realize our full potential. If we resist His help, we can never hope to reach that goal. Wise men and women grow to be wise by listening and trying to improve themselves. They are never content with who they are today, but they always look forward to what they can become.

May I grow a little bit today, and every day to come, Almighty God. Let me keep my ego in its place, never refusing to hear the things I should hear, in order that I might improve myself. Amen.

∽

It is His business to lead, command, impel, send, call, or whatever you want to call it. It is your business to obey, follow, move, respond, or what have you.

JIM ELLIOT

GIVING AND TAKING

The liberal soul shall be made fat: and he that watereth shall be watered also himself. He that withholdeth corn, the people shall curse him: but blessing shall be upon the head of him that selleth it.
PROVERBS 11:25–26

A long, terrible drought befell a certain kingdom. As it prolonged, the king began to fear that he and his family might suffer. He began to hoard the grain that was grown and imposed harsh taxes on the people. Each time he took food from the mouths of his subjects, however, he caused them to grow more angry and resentful. Finally the people rebelled against the selfish king, and they killed not only him but his family as well.

God wants us to be giving and loving in the bad times as well as in the good. Kindness should not be conditional on whether or not it is convenient. A giving person is well loved and reflects the kind of love that Christ came to spread upon this earth. Both Old and New Testaments give us the rule we should follow when we are asked to give: "Do unto others as you would have them do unto you." If we will begin to share what we have, we will be rewarded by our Father who sees all things that we do.

Make me a giving person, Almighty God. Keep the example of Christ firmly planted in my mind. Show me ways that I might give to others who are in need, and open my heart to them. Amen.

∽

Give freely to him that deserveth well, and asketh nothing: and that is a way of giving to thyself.

THOMAS FULLER

A FATHER'S INSTRUCTION

A wise son heareth his father's instruction:
but a scorner heareth not rebuke.

PROVERBS 13:1

It seemed like his father was always picking on him about something. "Do this." "Do that." There was never a time when he left him alone. Sometimes the boy thought it would be better if he didn't have a father. He couldn't get away with anything, and if he got caught doing something he wasn't supposed to, his old man was on his back in a flash. It wasn't fair.

When the boy grew up and had a family of his own, he realized that his father had kept after him to teach him how to live properly. He hadn't been so tough; in fact, there were times when he wondered how his dad had ever kept from being tougher. He wished there were some way to thank his father, but he decided the best way was to be a good father to his own kids.

Often we scorn instruction and rebuke because it isn't what we want to hear. But there comes a time when we are glad that we had the instruction. The words come echoing back to us, and we begin, at long last, to understand why they were offered. Too often we reject the words without actually paying attention to them. We need to listen to instruction no matter how much we don't want to hear it. It takes maturity to realize that others may know what is best for us. In God's case, no one could ever know anything better than He does.

Break my resistant spirit, O Lord. Help me to open myself to Your wise counsel. Lead me in the paths that I need to walk, and be patient as I learn to listen. Guide and protect my steps, Father. Amen.

∽

Above all, believe confidently that Jesus delights in maintaining that new nature within you, and imparting to it his strength and wisdom for its work.

ANDREW MURRAY

WHAT'S YOUR POTENTIAL?

Poverty and shame shall be to him
that refuseth instruction: but he that
regardeth reproof shall be honoured.
PROVERBS 13:18

A man who was very successful in business was asked what his secret was. He answered, "I never think I know everything. I'm always ready to listen to a new idea, and I always want to know when I'm doing something wrong." For forty years, he had been a top financial consultant, and he had a reputation for listening to even the youngest of colleagues. He never defended himself when he was rebuked by his superiors. He merely listened to the comment and did his best to improve.

This is the kind of spirit God wants in His children. God wants each one of us to grow to our full potential. Jesus tells us that we should be perfect as God Himself is perfect. The only way we can hope to move in that direction is to open ourselves to the constructive comments and criticisms of others. People can see from the outside things we might miss from the inside. Having the integrity and wisdom to seek out the counsel of others shows a definite desire to grow. We can do little else that is so pleasing to God. Only a fool refuses to listen to the observations of others. That person is too insecure to listen and too self-centered to want to grow.

Dear heavenly Father, bless me that I might grow to my full potential. Inspire me by Your Word and by the example of Your Son, Jesus Christ. Fill me with Your Spirit so that I may more closely resemble You in all that I do. Amen.

Criticism may not be agreeable, but it is necessary. It fulfills the same function as pain in the human body. It calls attention to an unhealthy state of things.

WINSTON CHURCHILL

HUMILITY AND CONCEIT

The fear of the LORD is the instruction
of wisdom; and before honour is humility.

PROVERBS 15:33

There was an actor who was fond of telling everyone how wonderful he was. His house was a museum of memorabilia from his career. His rave reviews were framed and hung in every room. Awards graced shelves and tables, and copies of his movies were played on large screens whenever visitors came by. He took such delight in rattling off his achievements that no one else ever felt compelled to praise him.

Too often people seek after honors when they should be striving after humility. Honors are not something that we deserve. They are gifts and should be given by others, not by ourselves. When we praise our own efforts, we slip into the sin of conceit. God is most pleased when we commit ourselves to doing what is right. Even if no honors come to us in this life, God will honor us richly in the life to come.

It is the humble man who is able to keep his sights set on God and in doing His will. If we use our time doing the things that God has asked of us, we will not have time to brag about our accomplishments. God has given us plenty to keep us busy all the days of our lives. If we stay committed to doing what is pleasing in His sight, He will bless us all our days.

Keep me humble, Lord. Help me to remember that I am nothing without You. You have given me everything I have and everything I am. You have blessed me with so many wonderful things, and I praise You. Amen.

∽

It is good for me, Lord, that Thou hast humbled me, that I may learn Thy righteous judgements, and may cast away all haughtiness of heart and all presumption.

THOMAS À KEMPIS

PROMISES, PROMISES

*In all labour there is profit: but the
talk of the lips tendeth only to penury.*
PROVERBS 14:23

The politician promised so many wonderful things. His constituents wanted to put their faith in him. They kept hoping someone would come along who cared about their plight. Every time new promises had been made, the hopes of the people soared. Each time, though, their hopes were dashed to the ground, and the great talk dissolved into wind. This time they hoped it would be different. They had to hold on to something. Promises were the best they could find. If even half the talk resulted in action, they would be a great deal better off than they were now.

Talk without action can be destructive. If we make a promise, we must be committed to following through. Jesus told the people of His day that they should not swear, because when they didn't do what they said, it was a sin. It is good for us to commit ourselves to helping other people, but when we make empty promises, we are being cruel and unloving. It is through actions, not mere words, that we show how much we care. Actions speak louder than words, and actions done in love speak the truth of Christ in our lives. Let us always strive to follow the example of Christ, saving our words until we are ready to act.

You have given me so much, O Lord, let me now share it with those who need it. Let not my words be a trap for me, but let me act in a way pleasing to You. There is nothing that needs to be said; only love needs to be shown. Amen.

In prevailing prayer, a child of God comes before Him with real faith in His promises and asks for things agreeable to His will, assured of being heard according to the true intent of the promises; and thus coming to God, he prevails with Him.

CHARLES FINNEY

THE PRICE OF PEACE

A soft answer turneth away wrath:
but grievous words stir up anger.
PROVERBS 15:1

The man had always lived by the adage "Fight fire with fire." He was truly a fighter. No one ever got the best of him. He'd seen his share of scuffles, but he did all right. His brother had always been a namby-pamby kindheart who thought peace should be kept at any cost. He hated how his brother would swallow his pride in order to keep the peace. He knew that he would never do that. That was the coward's way out. It was much better to let everybody know you weren't going to be pushed around. They wouldn't give you any trouble then.

One of the big problems in the world today is that everyone wants to show the rest of the world who is boss. No one wants to back off or work for peace. Each party wants to prove to the other that they are the most right. As long as we refuse to negotiate or compromise, we will have fighting. The desire of God is that we will learn to use kindness and love in order to solve our problems. A wisely spoken word could save much unpleasantness if only we will take the time to think before we act. Nothing good comes from stirring up the anger of our opponents, but there is much to be gained through kindness and common sense.

Soften my heart and the words of my mouth, dear God. Let me be a peacemaker, rather than an agitator. Let my words spread comfort and calm, and make my actions a testimony to Your great love. Amen.

To be of a peaceable spirit
brings peace along with it.
THOMAS WATSON

Happiness Is. . .

A merry heart maketh a cheerful countenance:
but by sorrow of the heart the spirit is broken.
Proverbs 15:13

You never get mad. You always seem to be happy and having a good time. I don't understand it. I wish I could be like you." The two walked along the beach together.

"It's really not that hard. You just have to decide that you're going to be happy, then do it. I got tired of being unhappy about everything, so I decided to quit," the other answered.

"It can't be that easy. There has to be more to it."

"It was that easy for me. I just thought about which I liked better; being happy or being sad. I don't like being sad, so I fight it."

We can decide to be happy. It takes work, but it is a conscious effort anyone can make. God is the giver of the greatest joy a person can ever know. When we make Him the Lord of our life, He can fill us with this unspeakable joy. All we need to do is ask Him in. When we are filled with sorrow, we break the spirit and undercut the effectiveness of Christ in our lives. The Lord dwells in joy, and He is well at home in a heart that is happy. When we are truly filled with joy, the whole world can see it. They will notice that we are not like everyone else, and there is no more powerful testimony to the power of God than a smile that cannot be taken away.

Fill my heart with Your joy, O Lord. Change the light of my countenance to happiness so that everyone will know the effect You have had on my life. Wherever I go, help me to spread joy and love. I praise You for Your gracious gift. Amen.

Jesus promised His disciples three things:
They would be completely fearless,
absurdly happy, and in constant trouble.
G. K. CHESTERTON

THE PRESENCE OF THE FATHER

He that spareth his rod hateth his son: but he that loveth him chasteneth him betimes.

PROVERBS 13:24

Everyone envied Jim. His father allowed him to do anything he wanted. He wasn't expected to do any work, he never had a curfew, and he got just about everything he asked for. His father never yelled at him, and he never got into trouble. He seemed to have everything he could want. That's why it came as such a surprise when he ran away from home.

When they finally found him, he told his friends he couldn't take it anymore. He knew his father didn't love him or care what happened to him. What had seemed so good to all Jim's friends turned out to be torture for Jim.

We need guidance and instruction. There are times when we wish we didn't have to have it, but it is vital for us to grow. God gives us instruction out of love for us. We might think that it would be easier if God didn't give us His law, but eventually we would feel abandoned and unloved. God knows what is best for us in every situation, and we know of His love because He is with us to guide us every step of the way. We would be completely lost if we could not feel God's presence in our lives—but we never have to worry about that happening.

O Lord, I thank You for Your presence in my life. Though I often do not want to be told what I should do, I know that Your Word is given out of love and concern for me. Make me open to Your instruction. Amen.

In the rush and noise of life, as you have intervals, step home within yourselves and be still. Wait upon God, and feel His good presence; this will carry you evenly through your day's business.

WILLIAM PENN

MONEY ISN'T
EVERYTHING

*Better is a little with righteousness
than great revenues without right.*
PROVERBS 16:8

It hadn't always been like this. When he had first started in business, he could sleep like a baby. He didn't have a care in the world. Now it was different. He tossed and turned every night because of the guilt he felt. He was short-tempered and angry all the time. He felt like a heel every time he foreclosed a mortgage. He had worked so long to get where he was, but there was no satisfaction to it, only turmoil. All the money and prestige in the world wouldn't make up for what he was feeling inside. He decided that the only way to deal with it was to quit his job. It was the best decision he ever made.

Sometimes we feel like money will make everything all right. We think that it can cure all our ills and make us whole. There are some things that money cannot do. It cannot give us peace of mind, and it cannot replace human relationships. We need other people, and we must love them more than money. When we serve money instead of people, we lose our sense of all that is right and good. It is much better to have little money and great happiness than to have mountains of money and no peace of mind.

Lord, I have what I need. Please make me content with that so that I don't go running off, pursuing things I do not need. Make me content with my life as it is, keeping me from dreaming of things that are really unimportant. Amen.

God divided the hand into fingers
so that money could slip through.
MARTIN LUTHER

STEADFAST DISCIPLINE

He that is slow to anger is better than the mighty;
and he that ruleth his spirit than he that taketh a city.

The choice came down to two salesmen. The first got great results, but he was a little bit wild, and he couldn't always be counted on. The second man got average results, but he could be counted on every time. The account was important, and they really wanted the best person to go after it. The first man figured he would be selected, while the other man only hoped. It came as a surprise to them both when the second man was selected. It was decided that dependability was more important than a smooth come-on.

God requires His followers to be disciplined. If we learn to practice self-control, we are well on the road to wisdom. It is not always easy to be a Christian, but we are expected to hold fast to the faith through bad times as well as good. The disciplined person learns to deal with hardship and, through discipline, gains endurance. God loves the person who is steadfast and unyielding in faith. The person who gives up easily and forgets their trust has no place with God. We need to pray for strength in our faith and trust that God will grant it. Discipline is greater than strength or intelligence or charm. It gives us the foundation we need to build a faith which cannot be shaken.

Give me a faith that will never fail, O Lord. I put my trust in You, because there is nothing on earth which is more powerful than Your might. Be with me to strengthen me and give me peace. Amen.

Consider the postage stamp: Its usefulness consists in the ability to stick to one thing till it gets there.

JOSH BILLINGS

COUNT ON ME

*A friend loveth at all times, and
a brother is born for adversity.*
PROVERBS 17:17

The man couldn't believe it. He had worked for the same company for almost thirty years, and suddenly they pulled the rug out from under him. He had never known anything else. It seemed like all his hard work had been for nothing. He had been a good employee, and he had never made trouble. Now he felt ashamed for no good reason. He didn't know what he would do.

A knock at the door brought him out of his deep thought, and he got up to answer it. Outside, his brother waited for him. When he saw his brother standing there, tears came into his eyes. Whenever anything had ever gone wrong, his older brother had been there to make him feel better. Just seeing him stand there made him feel like there was nothing to worry about. No matter what happened, he knew he could always count on his brother. He had yet to face any bad situation without his brother to support him, and as long as he could lean on him, he knew everything would be just fine.

As children of God, we can be thankful that we have Christ to call a brother. He will be with us in every situation, good and bad. He will be our support and our counselor. He will listen without judging, and He will never leave us. He is as true as any brother could be, and we can count on Him to be there for us no matter what.

*Heavenly Father, thank You for being there
when I need You. You are my strength and my
shield. I am so grateful for Your love. Amen.*

When I am with God my fear is gone;
in the great quiet of God my troubles
are as the pebbles on the road,
my joys are like the everlasting hills.
WALTER RAUSCHENBUSCH

THE STRENGTH OF THE LORD

*The name of the LORD is a strong tower:
the righteous runneth into it, and is safe.*

PROVERBS 18:10

The fort was just a mile ahead. The troops knew that if things got bad, they could retreat to its safe walls. Battle could be frightening, even to the point of despair, but there was special comfort, an invincibility, in being so close to a fort. At the sound of the trumpet, the doors would open and there would be comfort and refuge. Let the enemy come. It wouldn't do them any good. The tower of the sentry rose up above the hills, and it was a symbol of strength to every man on the field.

God is that fortress which is always close by. In times of struggle or chaos, we can turn and run to our strength and safety, which is the Lord. He will always be there, waiting with open arms, to receive His children who run to Him from the storm of battle. He is quick to comfort, and will ever defend His own. In His arms we are invincible. There is no force on earth that can touch us. The devil may fling his fiery darts, but they cannot penetrate the walls of God's great love. The world may batter at the door, but it will exhaust itself in the face of such a solid obstacle. Nothing can intrude upon the fortress of the Lord. Once inside His powerful protection, we are safe and sound for all time.

Lord, I come to You from the field of battle. I am weary and weak. I need Your protection and care. In Your love I can rest secure and know that everything will be alright. Open the gate of Your love to me now, O Lord, and grant me the safety I so long for. Amen.

∽

The same God who guides the stars in their courses, who directs the earth in its orbit, who feeds the burning furnace of the sun, and keeps the stars perpetually burning with their fires—the same God has promised to supply thy strength.

CHARLES SPURGEON

THE WISDOM OF WORDS

Death and life are in the power of the tongue:
and they that love it shall eat the fruit thereof.
PROVERBS 18:21

Pilate looked out over the crowd. So, it had come to this. People who usually had no use for him were now coming to him, looking for him to pass judgment on one of their own. It was exhilarating to have such power. With a word, he could bestow life or death. The Nazarene seemed totally unimpressed by his power, but the crowd knew better. They knew that his word was law! No matter how many times he was called upon to pronounce sentence, he still grew tense with excitement. This was power, and he loved it.

There is power in our words. Our tongues are like two-edged swords. They can protect and defend or cut down and destroy. We are in control of them. Sadly, many people act as though their tongues control their minds. As Christians, it is vital that we learn to control our tongues. James compares the tongue to a rudder. When a rudder is left untended, the ship flounders. Likewise, when our tongues move uncontrolled, the result is disaster. A wise person keeps a firm control over his or her words. Only words of life and light should be spoken, and with God's help we can hope to always have such graceful speech.

O Lord, take control of the rudder and steer this humble vessel. Use the words of my mouth to minister to the needs of others. Let the will of my heart always precede the words of my mouth. Amen.

∽

Peter was upon all occasions the mouth of the rest, not so much because he had more of the Master's ear than they, but because he had more of a tongue of his own; and what he said was sometimes approved and sometimes reprimanded—the common lot of those who are swift to speak.

MATTHEW HENRY

THE GRAND DESIGN

The hearing ear, and the seeing eye,
the LORD hath made even both of them.
PROVERBS 20:12

He stood looking on in awe. His son, his firstborn, was coming into the world, and he was a part of it. He stood by his wife's head, and together they shared the wonder of the experience. He had often doubted whether God existed, but now all of his doubts were gone. He looked on at the perfect little creation. Each finger and toe was a testament to God's loving existence. The miracle of life was overwhelming. It was inconceivable that something like this could happen by chance. Only a master artist of incomprehensible power and glory could come up with something so fine as human life.

When we look at God's creation, it is difficult to question anything about Him. There is so much to wonder at in the world. As we learn more and more, it should not make us skeptical of God. Quite the contrary, it should convince us that there is a grand Author to all creation, and that His power is far beyond our wildest imagination. To see God, all we must do is open our eyes and look around. Only a foolish person would deny God's existence in the face of such remarkable evidence. His signature is on each one of his creations. He is right there for the person who has eyes to see and ears to hear. God is all around us.

O Lord, You are indeed everywhere. I look to the sky, and Your beauty and wonder meets my eye. I look around, and I see You in the faces of those I meet. I look inward, and thankfully, I see You in my heart. Amen.

What can be more foolish than to think that all this rare fabric of heaven and earth could come by chance, when all the skill of science is not able to make an oyster?

JEREMY TAYLOR

THE AGE OF WISDOM

The glory of young men is their strength:
and the beauty of old men is the grey head.
PROVERBS 20:29

A famous ball player reflected over a highly successful career. He had been a feared hitter, and no one challenged his throwing arm from the field. He was well-muscled and a fine athlete. He quit playing while he was still doing well, and it was a decision he felt good about the rest of his life. When he had gotten old, he still had fine memories of his glory days, but that wasn't all he had. He had seen too many players who lived in their own pasts, and that was sad. He had used his time well, made good investments, developed other interests, and he enjoyed a full and active life as a senior citizen. His strength had faded and his athletic days were behind him, but he had his mind, and no one could take that away from him.

Often we judge younger men by their physical abilities, while we judge older men by their wisdom. Age brings with it certain limitations, but it also gives certain strengths. Experience gives us a perspective on life that we can obtain no other way than by growing older. The aged in our world have a wonderful legacy to offer us in the form of their experience and observations. They have walked a road that we are only beginning. Through their words, we may come to know the traps that lie along the way, and they can help us over them, if we will only let them.

Lord, let me respect those who have lived longer than I have. Open my heart to their instruction, and let me revere them the same way that I revere You. Amen.

The great thing about getting older is that you don't lose all the other ages you've been.
MADELEINE L'ENGLE

A GOOD NAME...

A good name is rather to be chosen than great riches,
and loving favour rather than silver and gold.
The rich and poor meet together: the LORD is
the maker of them all.

PROVERBS 22:1–2

Everyone loved Mr. B. He was a friendly old man who loved to play with children. Rumor had it that he was a brilliant man who could have done anything he wanted, but one day he walked out on his high-paying job and he never returned. Instead, he stayed home, began playing with the neighborhood children, and that had been how he'd spent his days ever since. If a child was sick, he was right there to visit them. If a child was hurt, he was there first to offer aid. If the familiar ringing of the ice cream truck sounded in the distance, Mr. B. was the first in line, ready to treat the neighborhood children, no matter how many of them there were. His only purpose in life seemed to be to spread joy to the children he met. He never had a cross word, and he let them know that he loved each and every one of them. He was legend, and no one who knew Mr. B. ever had anything bad to say about him.

When we give of ourselves, we find out what it really means to be rich. Life takes on new meaning, and we are filled with a feeling beyond description. God put us all here, and it is wonderful when we work together to make this life a joy. People who live to love others are a blessing to the Lord. In those people we can understand what it truly means to be happy.

*Teach me what it means to be happy, Father.
You are the source of all that is good and right.
Let me dwell within Your love, and let me be a
channel for Your love in this world that needs it
so very much. Amen.*

Every gift which is given, even though it be small,
is in reality great, if it be given with affection.

PINDAR

DAVID'S MIGHT

A wise man is strong; yea, a man of knowledge increaseth strength. For by wise counsel thou shalt make thy war: and in multitude of counsellors there is safety.
PROVERBS 24:5–6

The story of David and Goliath is a comforting one. Its moral says clearly that might does not always make right. If we will use our heads, we can overcome seemingly impossible odds. There was no question that Goliath was more powerful than David, but David proved to be the better warrior in knowing how to use his head and his faith.

There are times we all feel like we don't stand a chance. We are overwhelmed by the immensity of our troubles, and they bury us under feelings of futility and despair. If we try to face these problems on our own, we will probably fail. The wise person seeks support in difficult times. There is no better place to turn than to the Lord. His counsel is solid and true, and He will support and strengthen us in every situation. The evil of the world is powerless in the face of His might. If we join forces with God, there is nothing on earth which can defeat us. Like David, we can rest assured that God will stand beside us. Through faith we can be made victorious over the most powerful forces on earth.

I am weak, Father, but I have no fear for I know that You are strong. I have nothing to fear in this life, so long as I listen for Your wise counsel and have the wisdom to heed Your loving advice. Be with me, I pray. Amen.

I do not pray for a lighter load,
but for a stronger back.
PHILLIPS BROOKS

HAVING HUMILITY

Let another man praise thee, and not thine
own mouth; a stranger, and not thine own lips.
PROVERBS 27:2

The quarterback stood before the reporters, giving them his views of the upcoming game.

"I really don't think we have much to worry about. We have prepared for this game, we have a stronger defense and a stronger offense, and I am definitely a better quarterback than my opponent. My statistics speak for themselves. I've outperformed him in every category. He's good, but I'm better."

The interview ended, the game was played, and it was an upset. The opposing quarterback threw rings around his adversary, and the words that had been uttered hours before were spread far and wide through all the major news services.

When we compliment ourselves, we open ourselves to disaster. Pride comes before the fall, the saying goes, and it is true. We cannot fall if we never set ourselves up above everyone else. We can have incorrect pictures of our importance. When we do something well, we should content ourselves with the appreciation of others and not fall into the trap of conceit and arrogance. God loves humility, and His blessing is upon all who will think more highly of others than they think of themselves. Our praise should be for God and for others, but never for ourselves.

Lord, teach me humility and grace. I too often think that no one else can do things as well as I do. I get a wrong picture of my importance. Put my life into perspective, that I might live as I ought to. Amen.

⚭

Pride is at the bottom of all great mistakes.
JOHN RUSKIN

A FATHER'S PROTECTION

There be three things which go well, yea, four are comely in going: a lion, which is strongest among beasts, and turneth not away for any; a greyhound; an he goat also; and a king, against whom there is no rising up.

PROVERBS 30:29–31

She felt safe when she was with her father. She remembered the time that the wolves came around. He had taken out his gun and shot them all. Everyone else in the town had been afraid, but not her father. He stood up for everything that was right and good, and if there was something that had to be done, he did it. That was just the kind of person he was. Whenever she came home, the same old feelings of safety and comfort were there. As long as her father was there, everything would be just fine.

It is comforting to know that in this harsh and hard world someone will stand up and not let anything happen to us. That is what faith in God is all about. When we come to know God, we realize that we are never out of His sight and that He will watch over us, protect us, and care for us all the days of our lives. This assurance turns our lives from burdens into joys. He has given us the gift of life; and it is a blessed gift, which He rewards time after time. His love knows no bounds, as evidenced by His greatest gift of all: the Christ, the Babe of Bethlehem.

My God, You are with me in all of the dark hours and hard times. I do not know what I would do without You. You give me so much, and when I am afraid, You comfort and support me. Thank You for being with me, Lord. Amen.

∽

"Hope thou in God" (Psalm 42:5). Oh, remember this: There is never a time when we may not hope in God. Whatever our necessities, however great our difficulties, and though to all appearance help is impossible, yet our business is to hope in God, and it will be found that it is not in vain.

GEORGE MÜLLER

31 Days with God
for Mothers
ISBN 978-1-60260-016-4

31 Days with God
for Grads
ISBN 978-1-60260-017-1

31 Days with God
for Fathers
ISBN 978-1-60260-018-8

ONLY 99 CENTS EACH!

AVAILABLE WHEREVER CHRISTIAN BOOKS ARE SOLD.